EAF
CARTHUSIAN
WRITINGS

EARLY CARTHUSIAN WRITINGS

St Bruno

Bl. Guigo

Guigo II

GRACEWING

First published by St Hugh's Charterhouse, Parkminster,
this edition published 2009

Gracewing
2 Southern Avenue, Leominster
Herefordshire, HR6 0QF

The right of A Carthusian to be identified as the author of this
work has been asserted in accordance with the Copyright, Designs
and Patents Act 1988.

ISBN 978 0 85244 689 8

CONTENTS

"Dies Natalis" 6ᵗʰ October 1101

'Bruno... a man who understood the heart.'
Bl Guigo I (Life of St Hugh)

OUR HOLY FATHER ST BRUNO TO HIS CARTHUSIAN SONS AT THE CHARTREUSE

Written from Calabria in the last years of the XIth century

to my BROThERS,

whom i love in christ

aBove everything else,

greetings from your

BROThER,

BRUNO.

HAVE HEARD FROM
ouʀ ꝺeaʀ Bʀotheʀ
Lanꝺuín a ꝺetaíleꝺ
anꝺ moꝭíng
account oꝼ how
ꝼíʀm you aʀe ín youʀ
ʀesolꝭe to ꝼollow a path
oꝼ líꝼe so commenꝺaBle anꝺ ín
accoʀꝺ wíth ʀíght ʀeason,
anꝺ haꝭe leaʀneꝺ oꝼ youʀ
aʀꝺent loꝭe anꝺ unꝼlaggíng
zeal ꝼoʀ all that peʀtaíns to
moʀal ʀectítuꝺe anꝺ the
ꝼullness oꝼ chʀístían matuʀíty,
anꝺ my spíʀít ʀejoíces ín the
loʀꝺ. í tʀuly exalt, anꝺ am
swept away By my ímpulse to
pʀaíse anꝺ thanksgíꝭíng; yet, at
the same tíme, í BítteʀLy lament.

I rejoice, as is only right, over the ripening fruit of your virtues; but I blush, and bemoan my own condition, since I wallow so listless and inactive in the filth of my sins.

Rejoice, therefore, my beloved brothers, over the lot of overflowing happiness that has fallen to you, and for the grace of god that you have received in such abundance. Rejoice that you have succeeded in escaping the countless dangers and shipwrecks of this storm-tossed world, and have reached a quiet corner in the security of a hidden harbour. Many would like to join you, and many there are also who make considerable effort to do so, but fail in their attempt. What is more, many are shut out even after having attained it, since it was not in the plan of god to give them this grace.

Therefore, my brothers, count it a certitude, proven time and time again: whoever has experienced such an enviable good, and subsequently lost it for whatever reasons, will grieve over his loss to the end of his days, if he has any regard or concern for the salvation of his soul.

As regards you lay monks, brothers, so close to my heart, I have only this to say: my soul glorifies the Lord, since I can perceive the glories of his mercy toward you from the account of your beloved father and prior, who boasts a great deal about you, and rejoices over you. I share in this joy, since God in his power never ceases to inscribe on your hearts, however little education you may have, not only love, but understanding. that is to say, when you are careful and zealous to observe a genuine

obedience, conceived not only as the carrying out of god's commands, but as the original key to the spiritual life and its final stamp of authenticity, demanding as it does deep humility and outstanding patience, as well as sincere love for the lord and our brothers, then it is clear that you are gathering with relish no less than the most delectable and life-giving fruits of holy scripture.

So, my brothers, abide in that which you have attained, and avoid like the plague that baneful crowd of would-be monks who in reality are as empty as can be, peddling their writings, and speaking in hushed tones about things they neither cherish nor understand, but rather contradict by their words and actions. they are lazy, and wander from place to place, slandering all those who are

conscientious and dedicated, and imagining themselves worthy of praise if they blacken the name of those who really are. to them, anything resembling discipline or obedience is loathsome.

As for our brother Landuin, i had intended to keep him here on account of his rather serious and recurrent illnesses; but he would have none of it, claiming that there could be nothing worthwhile for him, no health or joy nor zest for life, apart from you. with repeated sighs, and a veritable gushing fountain of tears for you, he laid before me how much you mean to him, and the unadulterated affection he bears for you in the lord. as a result, i have not wanted to force the issue, lest i cause grief either to him or to you, who are so dear to me for your maturity and excellence of spirit. wherefore, my brothers, i am

very serious in my request, at once humble and insistent, that you manifest by your deeds the love you bear in your heart for your prior and beloved father by kindly and attentively providing him with everything he needs for the various requirements of his health. he may be unwilling to go along with what your loving solicitude may dictate, preferring to jeopardise his life and health rather than be found lacking in some point of external observance. after all, this is normally inadmissible and he might blush to hold the first rank among you, and yet trail in these matters, fearing that you might become negligent or lukewarm on his account. yet, i hardly think there is any danger of that; so, i hereby grant you the necessary authority to take my place in this particular, and respectfully compel him to accept whatever you accord him for his health.

As for me, brothers, I would have you know that the only desire I have, after god, is to come and see you. As soon as I can, god willing, I will do just that.

Farewell.

OUR HOLY FATHER
ST BRUNO TO
RAOUL LE VERD

Written from Calabria in the last years of the XIth century

to my esteemed friend

raoul,

dean of the cathedral

chapter at rheims,

i, bruno, send my greetings,

as all my heartfelt

affection toward you bids

me

HE LOYALTY YOU
have shown
during our long
and mellowed
friendship is all
the more beautiful and
remarkable in that it is
only rarely found. for,
even though a great
distance and many years lie
between us, your kindly
sentiments have always been
with me. this is certainly clear
enough from your wonderful
letters, in which you have
professed your friendship
over and over again, and
from the many other
indications you

have given of it, including the favours you have so generously shown, both to me, and to Brother Bernard on my account. For all this, I give you my thanks, dear friend, not in a way which could ever be commensurate with what you deserve of me, but springing, at least, from the deepest source of sincere love.

I sent a messenger with a letter to you some time ago, one who had proved reliable on other occasions; but since he has not yet returned, I thought it best to send you one of the brethren. He can give you a fuller account of how things are here by word of mouth than I could ever do with pen and ink.

I assure you, first of all, that my health is good, thinking that

the news will not be unwelcome to you. I wish that I could say the same for my soul! the external situation is as satisfactory as could be desired; but I stand as a beggar before the mercy of god, praying that he will heal all the infirmities of my soul, and fulfil all my desires with his bounty.

I am living in the wilderness of calabria, far removed from habitation. there are some brethren with me, some of whom are very well educated, and they are keeping assiduous watch for their lord, so as to open to him at once when he knocks. I could never even begin to tell you how charming and pleasant it is. the temperatures are mild, the air is healthful; a broad plain, delightful to behold, stretches between the mountains along their entire length, bursting with fragrant meadows and flowery fields. one could hardly describe

the impression made by the gently rolling hills on all sides, with their cool and shady glens tucked away, and such an abundance of refreshing springs, brooks and streams. Besides all this, there are verdant gardens, and all sorts of fruit-bearing trees.

Yet why dwell on such things as these? The man of true insight has other delights, far more useful and attractive, because divine. It is true, though, that our rather feeble nature is renewed and finds new life in such perspectives, wearied by its spiritual pursuits and austere mode of life. It is like a bow, which soon wears out and runs the risk of becoming useless, if it is kept continually taut.

In any case, what benefits and divine exultation the silence and solitude of the desert hold in store for those who love it, only those who have experienced it can know. For here men of strong will can enter into themselves and remain there as much as they like, diligently cultivating the seeds of virtue, and eating the fruits of paradise with joy. Here, they can acquire the eye that wounds the bridegroom with love by the limpidity of its gaze, and whose purity allows them to see god himself. Here they can observe a busy leisure and rest in quiet activity. Here also, god crowns his athletes for their stern struggle with the hoped-for reward: a peace unknown to the world, and joy in the holy spirit.

Such a way of life is exemplified by Rachel, who was preferred by Jacob for her beauty even though she bore fewer children than Leah, with her less penetrating eyes. Contemplation, to be sure, has fewer offspring than does action, and yet Joseph and Benjamin were the favourites of their father. This life is the best part chosen by Mary, never to be taken away from her. It is also that extraordinarily beautiful Shunammite, the only one in Israel able to take care of David and keep him warm in his old age. I could only wish, brother, that you, too, had such an exclusive love for her, so that, lost in her embrace, you burned with divine love! If only a love like this would take possession of you! Immediately, all the glory in the world would seem like so much dirt to you, whatever the smooth words and false attractions she

offered to deceive you. Wealth, and its concomitant anxieties, you would cast off without a thought as a burden to the freedom of the spirit. You would want no more of pleasure either, harmful as it is to both body and soul.

You know very well who it is that says to us, 'he who loves the world, and the things in the world, such as the lust of the flesh, the lust of the eyes, and ambition, does not have the love of the father abiding in him'; also 'friendship with the world is enmity with god'. What could be so evil and destructive, then, so unfortunate, or so much the mark of a crazed and headstrong spirit, as to put yourself at odds with the one whose power you cannot resist and whose righteous vengeance you could never hope to escape! Surely we are not stronger than

he! surely you do not think he will leave unpunished in the end all the affronts and contempt he receives, merely because his patient solicitude now incites us to repentance! for what could be more perverted, more reckless and contrary to nature and right order, than to love the creature more than the creator, what passes away more than what lasts forever, or to seek rather the goods of earth than those of heaven?

So, what do you think ought to be done, dear friend? what else, but to trust in the exhortation of god himself, and to believe in the truth which cannot deceive? for he calls out to everyone, saying, 'come to me, all who labour and are heavy laden, and i will give you rest.' is it not, after all, a most ridiculous and fruitless labour to be swollen with lust, continually to be tortured with

anxiety and worry, fear and sorrow, for the objects of your passion? Is there any heavier burden than to have one's spirit thus cast down into the abyss from the sublime peak of its natural dignity - the veritable quintessence of right order gone awry? Flee, my brother, from these unending miseries and disturbances; leave the raging storms of this world for the secure and quiet harbour of the port.

For you know very well what wisdom in person has to say to us: 'whoever does not renounce all that he has, cannot be my disciple.'

Who cannot perceive what a beautiful thing it is, how beneficial, and how delightful besides, to remain in the school of

christ under the guidance of the holy spirit, there to learn that divine philosophy which alone shows the way to true happiness!

So, you must consider the facts very honestly: if the love of god does not succeed in attracting you, nor considerations of self-interest spur you on in the face of such enormous rewards, at least dire necessity and the fear of chastisement ought to compel you to move in this direction. for you know the promise that binds you and to whom it was made. it is none other than the omnipotent and awesome one to whom you consecrated yourself as a pleasing and wholly acceptable offering. to him it is not permissible to lie, nor would it do any good, besides; for he does not let himself be mocked with impunity.

You remember, after all, the time you and I, and fulk one-eye, were together in the little garden adjoining adam's house, where I was staying at the time. we had been discussing for some while, as I recall, the false attractions and ephemeral riches of this present life, and comparing them with the joys of eternal glory. as a result, we were inflamed with divine love and we promised, determined and vowed to abandon the fleeting shadows of this world at the earliest opportunity, and lay hold of the eternal by taking the monastic habit. we would, indeed, have done so forthwith; but fulk went off to rome, and we postponed our resolution in the expectation of his return. he was delayed, however, and other things got in the way as well, so that, in the end, fervour vanished, and resolve grew cold.

So, what is left, dear friend, but to absolve yourself as quickly as possible from the obligations of such a debt? Otherwise, you run the risk of incurring the wrath of the all-powerful for such serious and long-standing deception, not to mention the frightful torments that are its consequence. What potentate, after all, of this world would ever leave himself unavenged if he were cheated by any of his subjects of a promised gift, especially if he considered it to be of outstanding value? So, never mind me, simply listen to the psalmist, or rather to the holy spirit, who declares: 'Make your vows to the lord your god and perform them; let all around him bring gifts to him who is to be feared, who cuts off the spirit of princes, who is terrible to the kings of the earth.' It is the voice of the lord you hear - the voice of your god, the one who is feared

who cuts off the spirit of princes, who is terrible to the kings of the earth! for what reason does the spirit of god make such a point of this, if not to prod you into acquitting yourself of your vow? why do you find it burdensome since it entails no sacrifice or reduction of your goods and heaps up benefits rather for yourself than for the one who receives what you pay?

Do not let the deceptive lure of riches hold you back since they cannot remedy the real poverty of our soul; nor let your position detain you, since you cannot occupy it without notable jeopardy to the spiritual life. for, it would be repugnant and wicked indeed, if i may say so, to convert to your own use the goods of another, since you are, in fact, their steward and not their proprietor. in addition, if you should become desirous of

vaunting your wealth in empty show, and keep a large retinue for this purpose, will it not be necessary, in some way, to snatch from one person what you bestow with great largesse on someone else? your own resources, after all, would not suffice. yet such a procedure would be neither generous nor to good effect, for nothing can be considered generous which is not at the same time just.

You must also be careful not to be allured away from the exigencies of divine love in your attention to the needs of the archbishop. he has great confidence in your counsel and relies heavily upon it; but it is not always an easy matter to give advice that is both useful and just. it is rather divine love which proves itself the more useful, precisely to the extent that it is more in accord with right

reason. for what could be beneficial and right, so fitting and connatural to human nature as to love the good? yet what other good can compare with god? indeed, what other good is there besides god? whence it comes that the soul that has attained some degree of holiness and has experienced in some small measure the incomparable loveliness, beauty, and splendour of this good, is set on fire with love and cries out: 'my soul is thirsting for god, the god of my life; when shall i enter and see the face of god?'

My sincere hope brother, is that you will not spurn the counsel of a friend, nor turn a deaf ear to the words the holy spirit speaks (within). as my very close friend, i hope you will grant these desires of mine and put an end to my long vigil in your regard. otherwise, i will continue to be

tortured with solicitude, anxiety and fear for you. god forbid that you should die before acquitting yourself of your vow; for, in that case, you would leave me pining away with unremitting sorrow, without ever any hope of consolation.

My request, therefore, is that you will agree to go on pilgrimage to st nicholas, and from there make your way to us. thus, you will be able to see the one who loves you as no one else, and we will be able to speak face to face about our religious life, and how things are going, and whatever else might be a matter of common interest. i trust in the lord that you will not regret any trouble involved in such a journey.

This letter is not as succinct as it ordinarily ought to be; but that is only because I do not have the joy of your presence. As a result, I desired to prolong our conversation at least in writing, and thus have the pleasure of your company.

So, brother, stay in good health. Accept my ardent wish that you will take my words very much to heart.

BRUNO

PS. Would you send us the life of St Remigius? It is impossible to obtain it here.

Farewell.

THE CREED OF
ST BRUNO

DELIVERED ON HIS
DEATH BED IN 1101

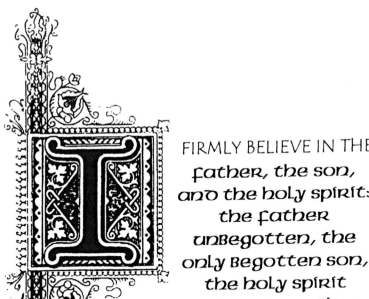

FIRMLY BELIEVE IN THE
father, the son,
and the holy spirit:
the father
unbegotten, the
only begotten son,
the holy spirit
proceeding from them
both; and I believe that
these three persons are but
one god.

Believe that the same
son of god was conceived by
the holy spirit in the womb of
the virgin mary. I believe that
the virgin was chaste before
she bore her child, that she
remained a virgin

while she bore her child, and
continued a virgin ever after. I
believe that the same son of god
was conceived among men, a
true man with no sin. I believe the
same son of god was captured by
the hatred of some of the Jews
who did not believe, was bound
unjustly, covered with spittle,
and scourged. I believe that he
died, was buried, and descended
into hell to free those of his who
were held there.

he descended for our
redemption, he rose again, he
ascended into heaven, and from
there he will come to judge the
living and the dead.

Believe also in the
sacraments that the church
believes and holds in reverence,
and especially that what has been
consecrated on the altar is the
true flesh and the true blood of
our lord Jesus christ, which we
receive for the forgiveness of
our sins and in the hope of

eternal salvation. I Belie.
Resurrection of the flesh u..
everlasting life.

I acknowledge and Believe the
holy and ineffable trinity, father,
son, and holy spirit, to be but only
one god, of only one substance, of
only one nature, of only one
majesty and power. we profess
that the father was neither
Begotten nor created but that he
has Begotten. the father takes his
origin from no one; of him the son
is Born and the holy spirit
proceeds. he is the source and
origin of all divinity. and the
father, ineffable By his very
nature, from his own substance
has Begotten the son ineffably;
But he has Begotten nothing
except what he is himself. god
has Begotten god, light has
Begotten light, and it is from him
that all fatherhood in heaven
and on earth proceeds.

amen.

THE LETTER OF BL GUIGO, FIFTH PRIOR OF THE GRANDE CHARTREUSE

Written in approximately 1135

to the reverend n.,

guigo

least of those servants of

the cross

who are in the

charterhouse

to live and to die for christ

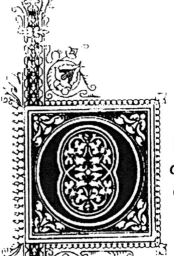

NE MAN WILL THINK another happy. I esteem him happy above all who does not strive to be lifted up with great honours in a palace, but who elects, humble, to live like a poor country man in a hermitage; who with thoughtful application loves to meditate in peace; who seeks to sit by himself in silence.

For to shine with honours, to be lifted up with dignities, is in my judgement a way of little peace, subject to perils,

Burdened with cares,
treacherous to many, and to
none secure. happy in the
beginning, perplexed in its
development, wretched in its
end. flattering to the unworthy,
disgraceful to the good,
generally deceptive to both. while
it makes many wretched, it
satisfies none, makes no one
happy.

But the poor and lonely life,
hard in its beginning, easy in its
progress, becomes, in its end,
heavenly. it is constant in
adversity, trusty in hours of
doubt, modest in those of good
fortune. sober fare, simple
garments, laconic speech, chaste
manners. the highest ambition,
because without ambition. often
wounded with sorrow at the
thought of past wrong done, it
avoids present, is wary of future
evil. resting on the hope of mercy,

without trust in its own merit, it
thirsts after heaven, is sick of
earth, earnestly strives for right
conduct, which it retains in
constancy and holds firmly for
ever. it fasts with determined
constancy in love of the cross, yet
consents to eat for the body's
need. in both it observes the
greatest moderation, for when
it dines it restrains greed and
when it fasts, vanity. it is devoted
to reading, but mostly in the
scripture canon and in holy books,
where it is more intent upon the
inner marrow of meaning than
on the spume of words. but you
may praise or wonder more at
this: that such a life is continually
idle yet never lazy. for it finds
many things indeed to do, so that
time is more often lacking to it
than this or that occupation. it
more often laments that its time
has slipped away than that its
business is tedious.

What else? a happy subject, to advise leisure, but such an exhortation seeks out a mind that is its own master, concerned with its own business, disdaining to be caught up in the affairs of others, or of society. who so fights as a soldier of christ in peace as to refuse double service as a soldier of god and a hireling of the world. who knows for sure it cannot here be glad with this world and then in the next reign with god.

Small matters are these, and their like, if you recall what drink he took at the gibbet, who calls you to kingship. like it or not, you must follow the example of christ poor if you would have fellowship with christ in his riches. if we suffer with him, says the apostle, we will reign with him. if we die with him, then

we shall live together with him. the mediator himself replied to the two disciples who asked him if one of them might sit at his right hand and the other at his left: 'can you drink the chalice which i am about to drink?' here he made clear that it is by cups of earthly bitterness that we come to the banquet of the patriarchs and to the nectar of heavenly celebrations.

Since friendship strengthens confidence i charge, advise and beg you, my best beloved in christ, dear to me since the day i knew you, that as you are farseeing, careful, learned and most acute, take care to save the little bit of life that remains still unconsumed, snatch it from the world, light under it the fire of love to burn it up as an evening sacrifice to god. delay not, but be like christ both priest and victim,

in an odour of sweetness to god
and to men.

Now, that you may fully
understand the drift of all my
argument, I appeal to your wise
judgement in few words with
what is at once the counsel and
desire of my soul. undertake our
observance as a man of great
heart and noble deeds, for the
sake of your eternal salvation.
Become a recruit of christ and
stand guard in the camp of the
heavenly army watchful with
your sword on your thigh against
the terrors of the night.

Here, then, I urge you to an
enterprise that is good to
undertake, easy to carry out and
happy in its consummation. let
prayers be said, I beg you, that in
carrying out so worthy a business
you may exert yourself in

proportion to the grace that will
smile on you in god's favour. as to
where or when you must do this
thing, I leave it to the choice of
your own prudence. But to delay,
or to hesitate will not, as I believe,
serve your turn.

I will proceed no further with
this, for fear that rough and
uncouth lines might offend you, a
man of palaces and courts.
an end and a measure then to
this letter, But never an end to
my affection or love for you.

"THE SCALE OF THE CLOISTER" BY GUIGO II, NINTH PRIOR OF THE GRANDE CHARTREUSE

Written in approximately 1150

to his well-beloved Brother

gervaise,

Brother guigo sends his

greetings, with the sincere

wish that he may delight in

the Lord.

O LOVE YOU, MY
BROTHER, I am
indeed bound, if
for no other
reason than that
you first loved
me; and to write
to you I am compelled,
because you have asked
me to do so in the letters
you have written to me.

have therefore decided
to send you certain things
that I have written on the
spiritual exercises of the
cloister, so that you (who
know more of these matters
from experience than I from
mere study) may be the judge

and corrector of my thoughts.

And it is but fitting that I should send you this, the first results of my toil, that you may gather the first-fruits of the young plant which you rescued from the service of pharaoh and a too-indulgent solitude, and placed in the army set in battle array; cleverly grafting on a cultivated tree the branch you cut from the wild olive.

I

One day, while occupied in manual labour, I began to think about a man's spiritual exercises. As I pondered the matter it occurred to me that there were four steps in the spiritual life came to mind: reading,

meditation, prayer and contemplation.

This is the scale of the cloister - a scale set between heaven and earth, having but few steps, but reaching an immense and unbelievable distance. For, while fixed upon earth, it pierces the clouds and scans the hidden places of heaven. You must know that as these steps are distinct in name and number, so they are in nature and order. If anyone shall consider the properties and claims of each one, what effect it has on us, how it differs from and excels another, he will reckon but trifling and easy the labour and time he spends in so doing, compared with the profit and pleasure he derives there from.

Now reading is a careful searching of the scriptures, with

an eye to the profit of the soul.
meditation is the studious
working of the mind, searching
for the hidden truths by the aid
of natural reason. prayer is the
devout turning of the heart to
god, in petition for the removal
of evil and bestowing of good.
contemplation is that raising up
whereby the mind is wrapt in
god, and tastes of the sweetness
of eternal joy.

ii

Having now described each of
the four steps, it remains to
consider the claims of each one
of them.

Reading, then, may be said to
seek the sweetness of the blessed
life, meditation to find it, prayer
to ask it, and contemplation to
enjoy it. hence the lord himself

says: 'seek, and you shall find: knock, and it shall be opened unto you.' seek by reading, and you will find by meditation. knock in prayer, and it shall be opened to you in contemplation. it is as if reading put the solid food into the mouth; meditation broke and masticated it, and prayer acquired the flavour, of which contemplation is the very sweetness which regales and delights. reading is the shell, meditation the kernel, prayer the entreaty of desire, and contemplation the delight in the sweetness attained.

That this may be understood more clearly, i will give one of many examples. in reading, i find: 'blessed are the pure of heart because they shall see god' - only a few words, indeed, but they are full of sweet meaning. these words nourish the soul as a grape nourishes the body, and after the

soul has carefully examined
them she says to herself: 'there is
something good here. I will
search my heart and see if
perchance I cannot find and
understand this purity. For
assuredly it must be a precious
and desirable thing, seeing that
those who possess it are called
blessed, and are promised the
vision of god; which is eternal
life, and which is praised in so
many places by holy scripture.'

Desirous therefore of
understanding this more fully,
the soul begins to chew upon this
grape, and to place it in the press.
then she encourages the reason
to find out exactly what this
most desirable and precious
purity is, and how it may be
obtained.

iii

Industrious meditation now comes along, and is not content to remain on the surface or cling to appearances, but searches deeper. It penetrates underneath and ponders each word. Meditation sees that it is not said: 'Blessed are the pure in body,' but 'Blessed are the pure in heart' - because to keep our hands from evil deeds is not enough if we do not keep our mind from evil thoughts. And this it finds confirmed by the authority of the prophet, when he says: 'Who shall ascend into the mountain of the Lord, or who shall stand in his holy place? The innocent in hands, and clean of heart.'

Meditation considers, too, how much the same prophet desired this purity when he said: 'Create a clean heart within me, O God,' and again: 'If I have looked at iniquity in my heart the Lord will not hear me.' It considers how carefully the Blessed Job kept his heart, who said: 'I made a covenant with my heart that I would not so much as think upon a virgin.' Behold how that holy man did violence to himself, who closed his eyes lest he should look upon vanity, lest he should carelessly see what he would afterwards unwillingly desire.

After having pondered this and similar things, meditation begins to think of the reward of this purity, how glorious and delightful it will be to see the beloved face of the Lord, more comely than the sons of men. He

will not be mean and lowly in the form with which his mother the synagogue clothed him, but will be clothed with the garment of immortality with which his father clothed him on the day of his resurrection and glory - the Lord's day. It considers how (in that vision) there will be the fullness spoken of by the prophet, when he says: 'I shall be satisfied when your glory shall appear.'

Now see how much juice has been squeezed from a little grape; how great a fire has come from so small a spark. Observe how the little lump: 'Blessed are the pure of heart, for they shall see god' has been hammered out on the anvil of meditation. (But how much more could it not be beaten out by one more versed in such things than I! For the well seems to me to be deep; but I, who am unskilled and a novice in such things, have scarcely been able to

draw forth the little that I have done.)

The soul, being now inflamed by these fiery brands and stirred by these desires, begins to perceive the sweetness of the ointment which has escaped from the broken alabaster-box; not yet indeed by the taste, but by the perfume. And from this she gathers how sweet must be the experience of the effects of this purity, of which even the meditation is so delightful. But what can she do? The soul burns with the desire to possess purity, but cannot perceive within herself the wherewithal to obtain it, and the more she seeks the more she thirsts. By adding meditation to meditation the soul adds sorrow to sorrow, because she thirsts for the sweetness which meditation shows lies in purity of heart, but which meditation does not taste.

For he who reads and meditates does not experience this sweetness unless it be given from above. To read and to meditate is common to both good and bad. The very pagan philosophers found by the light of human reason in what the highest good consisted. But when they knew god they did not glorify him as god, but presuming on their own powers said: 'we will magnify our tongue, our lips are our own: who is lord over us?' they therefore did not deserve to experience what they were able to see. They withered away in their thoughts, and all their wisdom was devoured - the wisdom which the study of human learning had given them; not the spirit of wisdom which alone gives the true wisdom, that palatable wisdom which rejoices and revives the soul with an unspeakable savour.

Of this wisdom it is said: 'wisdom shall not enter into a malicious soul.' this wisdom is from god alone. (he gave the duty of baptising to many, but the power and authority to forgive sins in baptism he reserved to himself. hence john figuratively and prudently says: 'he it is that baptises.' - and so likewise we can say: 'he it is who gives the taste of wisdom and makes the soul wise.') to speak is given to many, but to speak wisely is given to but few, for the lord distributes his gifts as he will and to whom he wills.

iv

And so the soul sees that of herself she cannot attain to the sweetness of experience and knowledge for which she longs,

and that the more high-minded she is the more is god exalted beyond her reach. the soul therefore humbles herself, and betakes herself to prayer, saying: 'o lord. who art not seen save by the pure of heart, i have examined in reading and i have sought in meditation how i can obtain true purity of heart, so that by means of it i may know you at least a little. i have sought your countenance, o lord, i have sought your countenance. long have i pondered in my heart, and in my meditation the fire has burnt up, the fire of desire to know you better.

Thou break the bread of scripture for me, and in this very breaking there is much knowledge. but the more that i know you the more do i desire to know you, not any longer in the dry husk of the letter but in the discernment of experience.

I ask for this, trusting not in my own merits but in your mercy. I acknowledge that I am unworthy, and a sinner; but even the little dogs do eat of the crumbs that fall from the table of their lords.

Grant me, o lord, a pledge of my future inheritance, just one little drop of heavenly dew wherewith to quench my thirst, for I burn with love.'

υ

By these and the like fiery words the soul inflames her desire and shows her affection. By these love songs she summons her spouse. and the lord, whose eyes are always on the just and whose ears are always open to

their prayers, does not even wait until her prayers are finished.

He invades the soul while she is yet in the midst of her prayers and hastens to satisfy her desire, inundated with the dew of heavenly sweetness covered with the fragrance of the best unguents. He banishes her weariness, satisfies her hunger, and quenches her thirst. He makes her forget all earthly things, wonderfully strengthening her, reviving her, inebriating her, and satisfying her with the memory of himself.

In certain carnal works the soul is so overcome by the concupiscence of the flesh that she loses all use of reason, and becomes as it were wholly carnal. So, too, in this sublime contemplation the carnal

motions are so absorbed and consumed that the flesh in no wise opposes the spirit, and a man becomes, as it were, wholly spiritual.

VI

But, o Lord, how shall we know when you do these things, and what sign will there be of your arrival? are sighs and tears the witnesses and messengers of this consolation and joy? if so, this is a new contrast, and an unusual meaning for these words. for what have sighs to do with consolation, and tears with joy - if indeed these are tears, and not rather an overflowing abundance of heavenly dew; the outward washing a sign of inward forgiveness. in the baptism of children the outward washing is a sign of inward absolution, but here, on the

contrary, the inward cleansing precedes the outward washing.

h happy tears, by which the inward defilement is washed away, by which the fires of sin are put out! Blessed are you who so weep, for you shall laugh. In these tears, o soul, recognise your spouse, and embrace your beloved. Now when thirst for joy burns you, suck milk and honey from the breasts of his consolation. These sighs and tears are the wonderful gifts and consolations of your spouse. In these tears he has given you drink in measure. These tears are your bread day and night: bread which strengthens the heart of man, bread sweeter than honey and the honeycomb.

Lord Jesus, if these tears which flow at the very thought

and desire of you are so sweet, how sweet will be the joy which the sight of you will give! If it is sweet to shed tears for you, how sweet it will be to rejoice in you!

But why do we speak of these secret things in public? why do we try to express these unutterable and indescribable effects of divine love in common words? those unacquainted with such things will not understand them, until they have read of them more clearly in the book of personal experience, until they have been taught by the unction itself. otherwise a mere reading of the words profits no one, for there is but little relish in reading the external words unless the inner meaning and gloss are found in the heart.

VII

O soul, we have been talking for a long while, for it is good for us to be here, and with peter and john to contemplate the glory of the bridegroom, and to remain with him awhile. should he so wish it, neither two nor yet three tabernacles would we build here, but one, in which we could all delight together.

But already the bridegroom says: 'let me go for the day is breaking.' already you have received the light of grace and the heavenly visitation for which you pined. the blessing has been given and the sinew of the thigh has been touched and withered, and the name has been changed from jacob into israel. in a short while the bridegroom will have

departed – so long desired, so quickly gone! He withdraws himself from sight, and from the sweetness of contemplation.

Yet he remains to guide and direct.

viii

But fear not, O Bride, and do not despair, or think yourself rejected, if for a while the Bridegroom hides his face. For all this will co-operate to your good, and from his coming and going you have much to gain.

He comes to you, and then he leaves you. He comes to console you, and leaves to put you on your guard, lest you become puffed up from the greatness of your consolation. He leaves lest, if

he be always with you, you begin to hold his company cheap, and to attribute this continual visitation not to grace but to nature.

FOR this grace must not be held as if one had any right to it, for the bridegroom gives it to whom he wills, and when he wills. It is a common proverb that familiarity breeds contempt. He departs therefore lest he be too continually contemplated, and that while absent he may be more ardently desired, and more fervently sought. For what has been long desired is found more gratefully.

Also, if the consolation of his presence were never absent (which presence concerns the future glory to be made manifest in us, seen now through a glass in a dark manner), we would

perchance think we had here an abiding city, and seek with less fervour the one which is to come. Lest therefore we deem this place of exile the fatherland, lest we deem the pledge as the whole sum, the Bridegroom comes and goes; now bringing consolation, now leaving us to our weakness. For a little while he allows us to taste and see how sweet he is, But Before we are fully satisfied he is gone again.

It is as if he hovered above us with wings outstretched encouraging us to fly. It is as if he were to say to us: 'you have tasted a little and seen how sweet I am, But, if you would be completely filled, run after me in the odour of my ointments, with heart uplifted to where I sit on the right of my father. there you will see me, not through a glass in a dark manner, But face to face, and your heart will be filled with

joy, and no one shall take your
joy from you.'

ix

But have a care, o bride! when
your bridegroom is absent, he is
not far away. you do not see him,
yet he always sees you. he is
covered with eyes, and can see to
the back as well as to the front,
so you can never hide from him.

Moreover, he keeps about you
his messenger spirits, like most
shrewd spies, so that they may
see how you behave while your
bridegroom is away, and tell him
if they see any signs of
wantonness or buffoonery in
you.

He is a jealous bridegroom, and
if perchance you look at other

Lovers, or attempt to please others more than him, he will straightway depart from you and seek another virgin bride. he (your bridegroom) is fastidious, and noble, and rich, and beautiful above the sons of men. he will therefore not deign to have any but a beautiful bride. if he should notice in you either spot or wrinkle, he will turn away his eyes, for he cannot stand any uncleanness. be therefore chaste, and be modest and humble, so that you may deserve to be visited often by your bridegroom.

fear that i have been a long while treating of this, but i was driven on by the abundance, as well as the delightfulness, of the matter. i have not drawn it out of my own will, but was led on in spite of myself, by i know not what attraction.

X

In order that what I have said at length may be seen better as a whole, I will recapitulate shortly what has gone before.

As has been pointed out by the examples given, it can be clearly seen that the aforesaid steps of the spiritual life hang together, and both temporally and causally follow from one another.

Reading comes first as the foundation; then meditation follows, working on the material supplied by reading.

Meditation seeks what is to be desired and, as it were, digs up the treasure and shows it. But

since of itself it cannot obtain the treasure, meditation sends us to prayer.

Prayer raising itself with all its strength to god begs for this desirable treasure, the sweetness of contemplation.

When contemplation comes, it rewards the toil of the first three, inebriating the soul with the dew of heavenly delight.

Reading, therefore, has to do with outward exertion: meditation with the inward understanding: prayer with the desire: while contemplation surpasses all the senses.

The first step is proper to beginners, the second to

proficients, the third to the devout, and the fourth to the blessed.

xi

These steps so hang together, and aid each other, that the lower ones without the higher are of little or no benefit, while the higher ones without the lower are seldom or never to be had.

For what avails it to spend the time continually reading, poring over the lives and writings of the saints? what avails it unless by turning them over in our mind and chewing on them we elicit the juice which, by swallowing, we take to the innermost places of our heart; so that from them we may be brought carefully to consider our state, and to

endeavour to imitate the lives of those whose deeds we love to read about. But how shall we be able to think of these things, and how shall we avoid overstepping (by meditating on vain and false things) the boundaries laid down by the holy fathers, unless we have been instructed first, either from books or by word of mouth? (for to listen pertains in a certain sense to reading, and so it is that we are wont to say we have read the books not only which we have read to ourselves or others, but also those which we have heard read by masters.)

Again, what does it profit a man to see by meditation what should be done, if by the aid of prayer he does not seek the grace of god to do it? for 'every best gift and every perfect gift is from above, coming down from the father of lights.'

Without him we are able to do nothing, but he himself works within us - yet not entirely without us, 'for we are god's coadjutors,' as the apostle says. god wishes that we should help him, that by giving our consent we should open the door of the will to him, standing without and forestalling us.

This same consent he demanded from the samaritan woman, when he said to her: 'call your husband,' as if to say: 'i wish to give you grace, but you must add the consent of your free will.' he demanded prayer from her when he said: 'if you knew the gift of god, and who it is that says to you: "give me to drink" you perhaps would have asked of him and he would have given you living water.' instructed by these words (as if by reading) the

woman meditated in her heart that it would be good and advantageous for her to have this water. Aroused, therefore, by the desire of having it, she betakes herself to prayer, saying: 'Lord, give me some of this water, that I may not thirst or come hither to draw.'

Now you can see how, first from hearing the word of the Lord, and then from meditating on it, she was led to prayer. For how could she have been desirous of asking, unless she had first been incited thereto by meditating? And of what use would meditation have been if prayer, coming afterwards, did not ask for what meditation showed was to be desired?

In order, then, that meditation may be profitable, it

must be followed by devout
prayer, of which the sweetness
of contemplation is the fruit.

xii

From what has been said it will
be seen that reading without
meditation is arid; meditation
without reading erroneous;
prayer without meditation tepid;
meditation without prayer
fruitless; prayer with the
devotion of contemplation,
satisfied; and the attainment of
contemplation without prayer
rare or miraculous.

God, whose power cannot be
reckoned or encompassed within
bounds and whose mercy is
beyond all his works, sometimes
raises up sons to abraham from
stones. sometimes he constrains
the hardhearted and unwilling

to desire his grace, and as a lavish father ('taking the Bull by the horns,' as they say) he pours himself forth when not asked.

But though we read that this sometimes happens to certain people, as, for instance, to paul and one or two others, yet we must not therefore presume on the divine indulgence, tempting god. Rather must we do what we can to dispose ourselves, By reading and meditating on the law of god, and praying to him to help our weakness and to look down upon our imperfection.

And this he himself teaches us to do, saying: 'ask, and it shall be given unto you: seek, and you shall find: knock, and it shall be opened unto you.' for 'the kingdom of heaven suffers violence and the violent bear it away.'

Now from the fore-given distinctions the nature of the steps can be clearly seen; how they are connected, and how they affect us.

Blessed is the man who is free from all other affairs, and desires only to occupy himself with these steps; who has sold all that he possesses and bought that field in which the most desirable treasure lies buried; who is still and sees how sweet is the Lord. Blessed is the man who is exercised in the first step, prudent in the second, devout in the third, and who in the fourth is lifted above himself, going from virtue unto virtue by these steps which he has set in his heart until he sees the god of gods in Zion. And blessed is he who in this highest step is allowed to tarry

for even a short time, who is able
to say: 'lo, i feel the grace of the
lord: lo, with peter and john i
contemplate his glory on the
mountain: lo, with jacob i delight
in the embraces of rachel.'
yet let such a one have a care,
lest, after being raised to the
very heavens, he fall with an
exceeding great fall into the
depths of the pit; lest, after
having seen god, he turn himself
to the lewd deeds of the world,
and the snares of the flesh. as
the human mind is weak, and
cannot stand for long the
brightness of the true light, it
should come down, quietly and in
order, to one of the three steps
by which it came up. it should rest
now on one and now on another,
according to the circumstances
of time and place, and the
disposition of the will; being the
nearer to god the further it is
from the first step.

Alas for the weak and miserable state of human nature! We see clearly by the light of reason and witness of scripture that in these four steps is contained the fullness of the blessed life and in them alone should a spiritual man be occupied. But who is able to keep to this rule of life? Who is he, and we will praise him?

To will is of many, to accomplish of few; and would that we were one of these few!

XIII

There are four obstacles to our being able to give our whole time to these steps; to state: unavoidable necessity, the benefit of good works, human infirmity and worldly vanity. The first is

excusable, the second tolerable,
the third miserable and the
fourth culpable.

It would have been better for
those ensnared by the fourth
obstacle had they never known
the glory of god than after
having experienced it to turn
back. what excuse can they have
for their sin? will not the lord
justly reproach them, saying:
'what ought i to have done for
you that i have not done? you
were not and i created you. you
sinned, and cut yourself off
from me, to become a servant of
the devil, and i redeemed you.
you fled round the world with
the impious ones, and i rescued
you. i have given you grace before
my eyes, and would have made
my dwelling with you, but you
despised me, and not only my
words but me myself have you
turned your back on, and gone
after your own desires.'

But, o good god, you are gentle and most merciful, a winning friend, a prudent counsellor, and a strong helper. how rash and how inhuman is he who rejects you, who turns so humble and so meek a guest from his heart!

O unhappy and pernicious exchange! to turn your creator from your heart, and to welcome vicious and harmful thoughts! to give over the heart which was until recently the privy couch of the holy spirit, which he visited with his heavenly joys - to give over that heart so suddenly to be trodden down by unclean thoughts and sins! are adulterous thoughts to be let in while the footprints of the bridegroom are yet warm? most unseemly and shameful is it to turn to tales and detraction the

ears which only lately heard
words not lawful for a man to
utter: to turn to the sight of
vanity the eyes so recently
washed with holy tears: to turn
to buffoonery, guile and
detraction the tongue which has
lately sung sweet love songs,
whose fiery and coaxing words
lately reconciled the bride and
bridegroom.

Far may such things be from
us, o lord! But if perchance
through human frailty we fall to
such a depth, let us not therefore
despair but let us hasten back to
the gentle physician, who raises
up the needy from the earth, and
lifts up the poor out of the dung-
hill.

It is now time to finish this
letter. Let us therefore pray god
that the obstacles which hinder

us from the contemplation of him may be diminished now, and completely removed in the future. May he lead us by the four steps from virtue to virtue, until we can see the god of gods in zion, where the elect enjoy the sweetness of divine contemplation - not drop by drop, not now and then, but (always filled by an unceasing flow of delight) having a joy that none may take away from them, and a peace that nothing can ever disturb.

And you, my brother, if it be ever given to you to ascend to the topmost of these steps, remember me, and pray for me, since all will then be well for yourself. So may we help each other, and he who hears will say: 'come.'

Lightning Source UK Ltd.
Milton Keynes UK
UKOW08f1929110517

300981UK00003B/109/P